AF291727

Low Sodium
Slow Cooker Cookbook

Easy and Prep-and-Go Recipes to Make in Your Slow Cooker (21 Day Meal Plan Included)

By Amy Clark

Table of Content

Introduction

The chances are you're reading this book because your physician has advised you to do so for health reasons. Either you have high blood pressure or following a health scare.

Well, don't get disheartened or scared. The great news is that by making healthy meals such as the recipes featured in this book, you'll be able to reduce your blood pressure in just weeks!

Not just that it's super easy to make the necessary changes to your diet. In this book, I'll show you how to reduce your sodium levels and improve your health in just a few easy steps.I've been a nutritionist for over twenty years and long before that I can remember learning to cook and bake with my mother. I love adapting tasty recipes to suit individual patients. But the best part of my job is seeing the results of my happy and healthy patients.

But first of all. Let's take a look at why you and/or your doctor may be concerned about your sodium levels. Sodium is not necessarily bad. We need it to live. Sodium is an electrolyte mineral which helps with water balance and muscle contractions. Just like fat, your doctor will never tell you to go on a no-fat or no-sodium diet.

The problem is when you consume it in large amounts. So, it's essential if you have high blood pressure to reduce your sodium to a safe level.

For Sue, with all my love!

Chapter 1 The Low Sodium Diet Basics

We all know that overeating salt is bad for us but what's the problem, exactly? This is a cookbook, and I am not going to bore you with pages and pages of science. This simple overview will give you the general picture, as to why we should cut down on salt and the damage it can do to our bodies. First and foremost, salt raises the blood pressure in our bodies, and this has various effects and manifestations for our health. In this Chapter, I'll introduce the basics of Low Sodium Diet. Now, Let's begin.

How Much Sodium Should You Consume?

Current recommendations are that Americans should eat around 1500-2300mg of sodium per day. But you can easily exceed your daily recommended amount just by having a breakfast cereal and lunch at a fast-food restaurant.

The problem with salt is it makes things taste great, and it's cheap. Manufacturers and fast food giants literally lace food with cheap salt. Sadly, they clearly care more about fat profits rather than the health of their customers.

However, with the recipes in this book, you'll find it easy to stick to these recommendations. And by aiming for a lower daily amount of sodium in your diet, you can expect to see results fast. In fact, your blood pressure can reduce in just two weeks.

Damaged Arteries

When your blood pressure is raised, this puts a strain on our arteries. And it's harder to pump the blood around our bodies. As a result, if you have had raised blood pressure for some time, your arteries will have to adapt to the job they need to do. They become stronger and thicker. But this is not a good thing because the space in the arteries become narrower.

Thus, it just makes your blood pressure even higher as blood is pumped through a smaller space. Eventually, the arteries either burst or clog – and then you have a big problem. The organs don't receive the nutrients they need; they become damaged, and often the result is fatal.

If the artery in question which bursts or becomes clogs is in the heart, then the result is a heart attack. A reduction in the blood reaching the heart results in frightening and painful angina.

If the artery in question is in your brain, then a reduction in blood supply can lead to dementia while a clot or blockage leads to a stroke.

I think it's fair to say that many of us will have witnessed first-hand, possibly with grandparents the devastation of such conditions. And obviously, everyone wants to avoid this life-changing, dangerous, and fatal health implications for themselves.

The great news is you can! And you can still eat great, tasty food.

How Does Potassium Work in Our Body?

If you have hypertension or high blood pressure, your doctor may have also told you to increase your potassium levels. In fact, reducing sodium and increasing potassium tend to go in hand in hand for two main reasons:

Firstly, potassium helps to lower your blood pressure by helping remove the adverse effects of sodium. And secondly, those who tend to overdo it on salty foods typically also under do it on potassium-rich foods at the same time. So, let's take a look at these both in a little more detail.

Potassium is a critical mineral which helps to lower blood pressure. Period. It works by helping your kidneys work more efficiently.

Your kidneys control your blood pressure and the amount of fluid stored in your body. The more fluid, the higher your blood pressure. Your kidneys filter your blood and remove excess fluid, urine. The process is controlled by a balance of sodium and potassium which sucks water across cell membranes. When you reduce sodium and increase potassium, you will have happier, healthier kidneys. They will work more efficiently and lower your blood pressure.

So that's the science part. When you overeating on pre-packaged and fast foods which are high in sodium - you are naturally foregoing healthier home-cooked meals typically containing potassium-rich foods such as fresh fruit and vegetables.

That's why those who have high sodium levels nearly always also have low potassium levels. The great news is that as you cut back on these processed junk foods - in favor of flavor-packed veggies cooked in your slow cooker - your potassium levels will soar. Awesome!

The adequate requirement of potassium for adults is currently 3,400 mg per day for men and 2,600 mg for women. However, the Office of Dietary Supplements is due to increase the daily value (DV) of potassium to 4,700 mg as of January 2020.

Below are some potassium-rich foods that you will find in my recipes. And can add to your diet either as snacks or in other recipes you make.

I'm not one for force-feeding people food they don't enjoy. So, take a look down the list along with helpful tips. Then pick out foods that you like and can quickly adapt into your diet and routine.

As long as you are not eating processed and fast food, you should be able to reach your recommended daily amount reasonably easily. There are so many foods on this potassium-rich list that I would challenge even the pickiest eater not to be able to make significant health changes.

Vegetables

All vegetables will give you a potassium boost, but these are some of the most potassium-rich ones.

- Potatoes (One medium baked potato delivers a massive 941mg of potassium! It's the perfect accompaniment to many of the slow-cooker meat stews and dishes in this book – and is a far tastier and healthier option than sodium packed and low potassium burger meal with fries).
- Broccoli
- Sweet potatoes
- Mushrooms
- Peas
- Cucumbers
- Zucchini
- Eggplant
- Pumpkins
- Leafy greens (you can easily get over 800mg of potassium in a 1 cup serving of spinach or other greens such as Swiss Chard).
- Tomatoes (tomatoes are easy to add to many dishes, and just ½ cup of tomato puree contains around 500mg of potassium).

- Bananas (just one banana contains over 400mg of potassium and is a filling and healthy snack).
- Oranges
- Cantaloupe
- Honeydew
- Apricots (just ½ cup of dried apricots makes a sweet snack full of fiber and contain over 1,100mg of potassium).
- Grapefruit
- Dried fruits, such as prunes, raisins, and dates (1/2 cup of prunes with your breakfast oatmeal or cereal delivers around 700mg of potassium).

Juices

Juices are also an easy way to get a sweet and healthy potassium boost. Just 1 cup of juice has the following amount of potassium:

- Prune juice 707mg
- Carrot juice 689 mg
- Passion fruit juice 687 mg
- Pomegranate juice 533 mg
- Orange juice 496 mg
- Vegetable juice 468 mg

Fish

A small 3-oz serving of the following fish packs a mighty potassium punch. You can even double up and have a 6-oz serve for double the potassium goodness:

- Atlantic Salmon 534 mg
- Mackerel: 474 mg
- Halibut: 449 mg
- Snapper: 444 mg
- Rainbow trout: 383 mg

Beans

Beans or legumes that are high in potassium include:
1 cup of beans contains the following amount of potassium:

- Kidney beans 607mg
- Lima beans 478mg
- Adzuki beans: 612 mg
- Cannellini beans: 595 mg
- Black beans: 401 mg
- Canned refried beans: 380 mg
- Lentils (if you like lentils then just 1 cup will deliver over 700g of potassium).

Other foods that are rich in potassium include:
Certain dairy products, such as milk and yogurt, are high in potassium. Choose low-fat options to keep cholesterol levels down.

- Milk (1 cup of milk contains around 350mg of potassium while 1 cup of yogurt has nearly 600mg).
- Salt substitutes (read labels to check potassium levels).
- Molasses
- Nuts
- Meat and poultry
- Brown and wild rice
- Bran cereal
- Whole-wheat bread and pasta

Lower sodium levels and higher potassium levels can also improve the effectiveness of any blood pressure medications that your physician has prescribed.

It is absolutely possible and to be expected to make significant improvements to your health stats in just a few weeks.

Maybe more so than in any other types of patients, there is far less upheaval for patients aiming to reduce their blood pressure by cutting their sodium levels than say, for example, a diabetic patient cutting carbohydrate.

And, many patients prefer their new style of eating and cooking. Instead of just adding too much salt and very little thought, they finally begin to experiment with delicious flavor-packed herbs and spices – and love the results!

Now let's take a look at "sodium culprits". And how by following my quick and easy changes to your diet, you will dramatically reduce your sodium intake. And thus, rapidly improve your health.

1 Table & Cooking Salt

First of all, simply throw out your regular salt and replace with a low-sodium salt. One teaspoon of salt contains 2300mg of sodium. That's about the top level you should be aiming to consume for one day. But simply changing to a low-sodium salt alternative will cut that in half!

2 Taste your food

The majority of people add salt to their food at the table. Now, that's fine if you have followed the first tip and have swapped to low-sodium salt. But I would still offer a few more tips here.

Now, many top-level chefs perfectly season and taste the food they prepare before it is served to you. Many of these chefs do not account for personal taste or differing taste buds. But consider customers that salt the food they have prepared, without first tasting it, as the height of bad manners and disrespect.

I, too, cook for people that pick up the salt shaker without ever tasting it, and I admit to a certain level of annoyance. So, first of all, it's not necessary to ban salt at the table but please, please, please, taste your food first and get out of the salt-everything-first-habit.

Stop and take a few bites to taste what is in your plate before you cover your food in salt. Taste, the meat, the potatoes, the vegetables and assess what the food tastes like first. Especially now that you are trying out new flavors and spices in your food, it might be that you don't need to add any salt. Or maybe just the potatoes are a little under seasoned for your taste.

3 Change your Salt Shaker

If you are a person that always adds salt to your food at the table, then consider investing a few dollars in a new salt shaker. What you are looking for in a new salt shaker is one that dispenses salt at a slower rate. Salt shakers tend to have larger holes than pepper shakers for larger salt crystals. But often they send salt pouring out of the shaker at quite an alarming rate. It's usually very easy to over-salt your food and add it far too liberally.

4 Measure Salt at the Table

Without getting caught up in stereotypes of domestic life, it can often be that one person is cooking the food in the home for the person that needs to reduce their sodium levels. So, after a loved one spends hours in the kitchen carefully measuring out low-sodium salt and flavorings. It's not particularly fair to undo all their hard work by just adding as much salt at the table, as though nothing mattered.

Now, I am not suggesting that you start measuring out quarter teaspoons of salt at the table. However, what you can do is measure out or use a pre-bought small salt shaker with a known amount of low-sodium salt. Typically, that might be 2 ounces or 50g or ten teaspoons. You'll be tasting your food by now, if you are following tip two on my list, so see how long it takes you to use an easy-to-measure amount of salt. You might mark a line halfway down your salt shaker that lets you know when you have consumed ten teaspoons of salt. This way you will know exactly how much salt you are adding at the table. And if this is an area you still need to watch.

5 Garlic Lovers

I happen to love garlic as do many people, and I know a lot of salt-addicts also adore garlic salt. Garlic salt can be sprinkled on most food if you love garlic, of course – whether it's meat and fish, soups, stews, carbohydrates or vegetables. Make your own garlic salt to add to your food by using one part low-sodium salt to two parts garlic granules. A one-quarter teaspoon serving of salt will come in at around 600mg of sodium. And it's a quarter of the maximum amount you should be aiming for in a day. Your low-sodium garlic salt quarter teaspoon serving will have just 100mg of sodium so you can afford to add a little extra.

6 Other Alternatives

The amount of salt in pre-packaged US food means it can be tough for Americans to buy regular food without it being laced with salt. There is salt in desserts, cakes, breakfast cereals, and just about everything you could think of. However, in addition to that, the US market is also renowned for giving Americans unrivaled consumer choice.

This is also true when it comes to low-sodium alternatives. There are simply hundreds of products available that will make flavoring your food with tasty options a breeze. If you replace your salt, stock cubes, sauces, seasoning mixes, and condiments with no or low sodium alternatives, you will have done most of what you need to do.

Let's take a look at the easy "sodium saves" you can make:

Food	Serve Size	Original /mg of sodium	Low-Sodium/mg of sodium
Table Salt	¼ teaspoon	625	325
Hot Sauce	One teaspoon	125	0
Chicken Broth	¼ cube	250	0
Beef Broth	¼ cube	250	0
Soy Sauce	1 tablespoon	290	70
BBQ Sauce	1 tablespoon	175	50
Tomato Ketchup (Heinz)	1 tablespoon	150	5
Baked Beans (Heinz)	8 ounces	800	550
Bacon	2 slices	385	200
Worcestershire Sauce	1 tbsp	165	135
Canned Tomatoes	½ cup	140	100
Parmesan Cheese	1 tablespoon	90	60
Tomato Sauce	¼ cup	240	15
Potato Chips	1 ounce	185	120
Canned chicken soup	10.5 ounces	350	140
Nuts	1 ounce	150	95
Hot Dogs	1 frank (2 ounces)	570	270
Sausage	3 ounces	500-1500	270
Monterey Jack Cheese	1 ounce	150	50

There's no need to stop dining out just because you need to follow a low-sodium diet. Follow a couple of tips and you can eat out several times a week.

i) Many family chain restaurants produce heart-healthy meals clearly indicated on their menus. They have carefully counted and labeled levels of fat, cholesterol, and sodium. Simply choose those!

ii) If you are dining in shall we say more sophisticated restaurants, then inform your server that you are on a low-sodium diet. And ask for your meal to be prepared without salt. Then salt your own meal with your brought along low-sodium salt shaker.

iii) Fast food restaurants are typically not the best place to frequent as most of the food is packed with cheap salt. But you can still order fries that are unsalted and burgers just plain with salad. Then add your own low-sodium ketchup, mayo, barbeque, and burger sauce. Do remember though that fries are still fried so are not the most heart-healthy food. So, keep these visits to treats and infrequent occasions.

8 Curry Love

The ultimate in tasty flavorsome food has to be curry. If you love curries, then my advice is to get experimenting. The flavor in curries comes from gently cooking blends of spices with onion and garlic for a fantastic base.

9 Preparation

You'll note that some of the recipes in this book include canned beans and vegetables. It's a far lower calorie option. But often the only option to have these types of produce preserved in brine or saltwater. Beans and vegetables are a heart-healthy food, but what about the salt in the brine?

Well, the good news is that laboratory analysis proves that rinsing the produce well can cut the sodium content by a quarter. So, don't miss out on fat-free filling foods that are great for the heart.

Slow cookers have many benefits in particular for those wanting to cut down on sodium. You know yourself that when you cook things for longer, the flavors have more time to develop. But we don't all have the time to stand around, stirring the food for hours. The slow cooker solves that problem. You can just walk away and allow the slow cooker to do its thing as those robust and rounded flavors develop.

When you use a slow cooker, the meat and vegetables have so much longer to take on the flavors of the herbs, spices, and broths you add. The flavor of the meat and vegetables amalgamate and become more intensified - and that's a great boon when you want to prepare fuller flavored dishes but with much less salt.

Not just that, typically, tougher cuts of meat are more flavorsome than quicker cooking cuts. When the meat fibers break down, you'll have delicious melt-in-the-mouth meat – and at a fraction of the price.

A slow cooker also has many other benefits. Even though a slow cooker is turned on for a longer time, they are more economical than other ways of cooking. So, you'll be helping to save the planet, in addition to making tasty, healthy meals.

What I also love is the fact that often you can just add the ingredients to the slow cooker in the morning with virtually no mess. And when you return in the evening after a long hard day at the office – your home is filled with delicious aromas, and your dinner is hot and ready to serve.

Before you get started there are a few do's and don'ts worth mentioning about this one-pot wonder. Follow these quick hints and tips to cook safe and healthy meals and to ensure your slow cooker remains in good condition:

Do: Make sure your cable is not underneath the slow cooker when cooking as this is a fire hazard.

Do: Read the manual

Do: Try not to lift the lid too often! Follow the recipe and stir as advised only otherwise you will let the heat out and slow down the desired cooking time.

Do: Check the recipe and use the right size slow cooker.

Do: Follow the recipe and layer the meat and vegetables as advised so that vegetables are at the bottom and have longer to cook than the meat.

Do: Brown meat as advised in the recipe as a slow cooker can't caramelize your meat and give it that extra flavor.

Do: Use lean meats in your recipe so that you are following low fat and a heart-healthy diet. Drain off any fat as advised in the recipe.

Do: Make sure the slow cooker is cool before you wash it to prevent it from cracking.

Do: Add tender vegetables, seafood, pasta, dairy products, and fresh herbs toward the end of cooking as advised in the recipe to prevent the food from becoming overcooked or from curdling.

Do: Use wooden, plastic, and rubber utensils when you stir.

Do: Cut vegetables such as sweet potatoes, carrot, swede, and potatoes evenly so that can cook evenly.

Don't

Don't: Put your slow cooker in the fridge. The ceramic pot is not designed to withstand cold temperatures and may crack. Empty leftover contents into fridge-safe containers and store covered. You can also freeze many dishes and reheat later.

Don't: Use your slow cooker to reheat food. The slow cooker is a cooker and is not designed to reach the correct temperatures to reheat food safely. Reheat leftover meals in a microwave, in a conventional oven, or a saucepan.

Don't: Cook food from frozen. Always use food that has been thawed to ensure that food is heated to the right temperature. Because the slow cooker heats the food slowly it can cause bacteria to grow,

Don't: Be afraid to experiment and try new things with your slow cooker. You can adapt your favorite recipes to cook in your slow cooker with a little thought.

Don't: Be afraid of cornflour. If your meal looks a little watery, then simply remove the lid and stir in some cornflour to thicken the sauce.

Don't: Add too much liquid. Follow the recipe carefully and don't have food swimming in water. A slow cooker has a closed lid, and so the moisture will stay in the slow cooker unlike when you cook on the stove, and the liquid can escape.

Don't: Overfill your pot. If you add too many ingredients and fill your slow cooker to the brim, it may have a hard time cooking it. You may return home after 8 hours to find the food is still not cooked as there isn't enough power to cook all the food through.

Don't: Add too much liquid. Slow cookers aren't the same as cooking on a hob, and all of the moisture that you add at the beginning will effectively stay in the pot because of the lid. Also, most foods tend to contain liquid which will cook out and add to the overall moisture of the dish.

How to Use This Book

As with any diet, you should check with your physician first. You will find that all the recipes are complete with calories, fat, protein, carbohydrates, fiber, sodium, and potassium. You can keep track of your sodium and potassium levels and aim to keep them within the guidelines detailed. I highly recommend that you keep a note of your blood pressure before commencing the diet. And then keep track of it as you follow the diet. As long as you lower your sodium and raise your potassium levels – you'll see incredible results FAST.

Best of luck.

Meal Plan	Breakfast	Lunch	Dinner	Side dish
Day-1	Apple Pie Oatmeal	Banana French Toast	Sweet and Sour Shrimp	Chocolate & Banana Bread
Day-2	Pumpkin Pie Oatmeal	Irish Soda Bread	Meat Loaf	Crab Dip
Day-3	Low-Cal Gingerbread Oatmeal	Crock Pot Breakfast Casserol	Salmon with Caramelized Onions	Walnuts Glazed in Maple Syrup
Day-4	Crock Pot Breakfast Casserole	Low-Cal Gingerbread Oatmeal	Fisherman's Stew	Ranch Mushrooms
Day-5	Irish Soda Bread	Pumpkin Pie Oatmeal	Fish Chowder	Buffalo Meatballs
Day-6	Banana French Toast	Apple Pie Oatmeal	Shrimp Creole	Buffalo Chicken Dip
Day-7	Grs with Baconeen Bean	Creamy Potato Soup	Veggie Soup	BBQ Chicken Sliders
Day-8	Coconut & Pecan Sweet Potatoes	Creamy Cauliflower & Butternut Squash Soup	Turkey, Wild Rice, and Mushroom Soup	Chocolate Chip Pan Cookies
Day-9	Veggie Bolognese	Crock Pot Turkey & Sweet Potato Chipotle Chili	Green Chili Stew	Chocolate Bread Pudding
Day-10	Bombay Potatoes	Beef &Barley Stew	Healthy Crockpot White Chicken Chili	Pineapple Dump Cake
Day-11	Potato & Broccoli Gratin	Healthy Crockpot White Chicken Chili	Beef &Barley Stew	Crock-Pot Zucchini Cake with Cream Cheese Frosting

Day-12	Summer Squash with Bell Pepper and Pineapple	Green Chili Stew	Crock Pot Turkey & Sweet Potato Chipotle Chili	Raspberry Almond Coffee Cake Recipe
Day-13	Slow Cooker Eggplant Lasagna	Turkey, Wild Rice, and Mushroom Soup	Creamy Cauliflower & Butternut Squash Soup	Rhubarb & Strawberry Crisp
Day-14	Slow Cooker Lentil & Vegetable Casserole	Veggie Soup	Creamy Potato Soup	Baked Apples
Day-15	Roasted Chickpeas	Sweet and Sour Shrimp	Crock-Pot Peachy Pork Chops	Ranch Mushrooms
Day-16	Basic Beans	Salmon with Caramelized Onions	Meat Loaf	Buffalo Meatballs
Day-17	Slow Cooker Red Beans & Rice	Slow Cooker Shrimp in Tomato Sauce	Short Ribs	Buffalo Chicken Dip
Day-18	Slow Cooker Butternut Squash & Parmesan Risotto	Fisherman's Stew	Beef Chimichangas	Walnuts Glazed in Maple Syrup
Day-19	Cheesy Spaghetti	Fish Chowder	Chicken Curry	Crab Dip
Day-20	Slow Cooker Wild Rice Pilaf	Shrimp Creole	Lemon & Herb Turkey Breasts	Baked Apples
Day-21	Bombay Potatoes	Creamy Mushroom and Broccoli Chicken	Apple & Cinnamon Spiced Honey Pork Loin	Raspberry Almond Coffee Cake Recipe

Chapter 2 Breakfast and brunch

Apple Pie Oatmeal

Prep time: 10 minutes, cook time: 4-6 hours; Serves 4

Ingredients:

- 3 medium apples, chopped
- 3 cup water
- 1 cup apple juice
- 1 cup steel-cut oats
- 1 tsp ground cinnamon
- 1 tbsp honey
- ¼ tsp ground nutmeg

Instructions:

1. Place all ingredients into a 4 to a 6-quart slow cooker, mix well and cover.

2. You can cook on LOW for 4 to 6 hours or on HIGH for 2 to 3 hours. Make sure to stir every hour or so to prevent sticking.

3. Adjust the sweetness by adding a little more honey or sweetener and serve immediately.

Nutrition Facts Per Serving:

Calories 320, Fat 4g, Carbs 66g, Protein 8g, Fiber 9g, Potassium 184mg, Sodium 7mg

Prep time: 20 minutes, cook time: 7-8 hours; Serves 6

Ingredients:

- 2 cup steel-cut oats
- 7 cup water
- 1½ cup pumpkin puree
- 1 tbsp pumpkin pie spice
- 1 tbsp vanilla extract
- ¼ tsp low-sodium salt

Instructions:

1. Place all ingredients into a 6-quart slow cooker, mix well and cover.

2. You can cook on LOW for 4 to 6 hours or on HIGH for 2 to 3 hours. Make sure to stir every hour or so to prevent sticking.

3. Adjust the sweetness by adding a little sweetener and serve immediately.

Nutrition Facts Per Serving:

Calories 338, Fat 6g, Carbs 60g, Protein 11g, Fiber 10g, Potassium 139mg, Sodium 113mg

Low-Cal Gingerbread Oatmeal

Prep time: 10 minutes, cook time: 4-5 hours; Serves 6

Ingredients:

- 1 cup steel-cut oatmeal
- 4 cup water
- ¼ cup molasses
- ½ cup brown sugar
- 2 tsp ground ginger
- 1 tsp ground cinnamon
- ½ tsp ground nutmeg
- ½ tsp ground cloves

Instructions:

1. Place all ingredients into a 4 to a 6-quart slow cooker, mix well and cover.

2. You can cook on LOW for 4 to 6 hours or on HIGH for 2 to 3 hours. Make sure to stir every hour or so to prevent sticking.

3. Serve immediately.

Nutrition Facts Per Serving:

Calories 205, Fat 2g, Carbs 45g, Protein 3g, Fiber 3g, Potassium 236mg, Sodium 17mg

Crock Pot Breakfast Casserole

Prep time: 20 minutes, cook time: 7 hours; Serves 10

Ingredients:

- 2 tbsp butter
- 1lb low-sodium breakfast sausage (cooked and drained)
- 1 onion, chopped
- 2 garlic cloves, minced
- 1 green bell pepper, chopped
- 1 4oz can green chilies or jalapeño peppers, drained well and chopped
- 2½ cup reduced-sodium Monterey Jack or Pepper Jack cheese, grated
- 18 eggs, beaten
- 1 to 2 tbsp chili powder
- ¼ tsp cayenne pepper, if desired
- ½ tsp low-sodium salt
- ¼ tsp black pepper
- Non-stick spray

Instructions:

1. Spray a 5-quart slow cooker with nonstick cooking spray.

2. Layer the sausage, onions, peppers, chilies, and cheese into the slow cooker.

3. Beat the eggs with the salt, pepper, chili powder, and cayenne and pour into the slow cooker.

4. Cover and cook on LOW for 7 to 8 hours.

Nutrition Facts Per Serving:

Calories 427, Fat 31g, Carbs 10g, Protein 27g, Fiber 1g, Potassium 361mg, Sodium 360mg

Irish Soda Bread

Prep time: 20 minutes, cook time: 2-3 hours; Serves 10

Ingredients:

- 2 ½ cup all-purpose flour
- 2 tbsp sugar
- 1 teaspoon baking powder
- 1 tsp baking soda
- ½ tsp low-sodium salt
- 3 tbsp butter, softened
- ¾ cup buttermilk
- Non-stick spray

Instructions:

1. Spray the inside of a 6 quart or larger slow cooker.

2. Mix the flour, sugar, baking powder, and salt in a large mixing bowl.

3. Rub the butter into the flour until the mixture resembles bread crumbs.

4. Stir in the buttermilk gradually until you have a not too sticky dough.

5. Knead the dough on a floured board for a few minutes until smooth.

6. Shape the dough into a round loaf and place in the slow cooker

7. Cut an X in the top of the loaf before covering.

8. Cook on HIGH for 2 to 3 hours until golden brown and the loaf sounds hollow when tapped.

Nutrition Facts Per Serving:

Calories 247, Fat 1g, Carbs 47g, Protein 7g, Fiber 2g, Potassium 107mg, Sodium 276mg

Prep time: 10 minutes, cook time: 2-3 hours; Serves 6

Ingredients:

- 12 1-inch thick slices from a whole wheat baguette
- 4 large eggs
- ¾ cup almond milk
- 1 tbsp coconut sugar
- 1 tbsp vanilla
- 1 tsp cinnamon
- 2 tbsp coconut oil, melted
- 2 bananas, sliced
- ½ lemon, freshly squeezed
- ½ cup chopped pecans
- Nonstick cooking spray

Instructions:

1. Spray a 5 to 6-quart slow cooker with nonstick cooking spray.

2. Arrange the bread on the base of the slow cooker.

3. Beat the eggs together with the milk, coconut sugar, vanilla, and cinnamon and pour over the bread.

4. Toss the banana slices with the lemon juice and arrange on top of the mixture.

5. Drizzle with the coconut oil and sprinkle with pecans.

6. Cook on HIGH for 2-3 hours until golden brown.

7. Serve with maple syrup if desired.

Nutrition Facts Per Serving:

Calories 273, Fat 9g, Carbs 42g, Protein 7g, Fiber 2g, Potassium 354mg, Sodium 173mg

Chapter 3 Broths, Sauces, and Condiments

Crock-Pot Cranberry Applesauce Recipe

Prep time: 15minutes, cook time: 4-6 hours; Serves 8

Ingredients:

- 10 apples such as golden delicious, peeled and roughly chopped
- 12oz cranberries, rinsed and drained

Instructions:

1. Place fruit in a 5-quart crockpot and mix well.

2. Cover crock-pot and cook on LOW for 4 - 6 hours or until everything is cooked and the fruit has dissolved into a sauce.

3. You can add sweetener if desired or use a blender if you prefer a less chunky sauce.

Nutrition Facts Per Serving:

Calories 113, Fat 0g, Carbs 28g, Protein 0g, Fiber 0g, Potassium 185mg, Sodium 1mg

Marinara Sauce

Prep time: 15 minutes, cook time: 3-4 hours; Serves 12

Ingredients:

- 10 garlic cloves, minced
- 1 14oz can no-added sodium diced tomatoes
- 1 14oz can no-added sodium crushed tomatoes
- 2 tbsp no-added sodium tomato paste
- 2 tbsp fresh basil, minced
- 1 tbsp onion powder
- 1 tbsp Italian seasoning
- 2 tsp balsamic vinegar

Instructions:

1. Place all ingredients into a 3 or 4-quart slow cooker and mix well.

2. Cover and cook on LOW for around 3-4 hours.

3. Serve with pasta, chicken, meat, and fish. The sauce keeps well for up to 2 weeks in a refrigerator and you can also freeze the sauce.

Nutrition Facts Per Serving:

Calories 292, Fat 0g, Carbs 6g, Protein 1g, Fiber 1g, Potassium 219mg, Sodium 116mg

Prep time: 5 minutes, cook time: 4 hours; Serves 10

Ingredients:

- 1 medium carrot, cut into 1-inch pieces
- 1 stalk celery, cut into 1-inch pieces
- 1 small onion, cut into 1-inch pieces
- 4lb skinless chicken leg quarters
- 6 sprigs fresh parsley
- 2 sprigs fresh thyme
- 1 bay leaf
- 1 garlic clove, minced
- 20 whole peppercorns
- 9 cup water

Instructions:

1. Place all ingredients in a 6-quart slow cooker.

2. Cover and cook on HIGH for 4 hours.

3. Leave to cool and then strain well.

4. Use the cooked chicken for other dishes. The strained broth is flavorsome and the perfect base for countless dishes yet is virtually calorie and sodium-free. The broth can be refrigerated or frozen.

Nutrition Facts Per Serving:

Calories 34, Fat <1g, Carbs 3g, Protein 4g, Fiber 0g, Potassium 145mg, Sodium 39mg

Blueberry Butter

Prep time: 15minutes, cook time: 5-6 hours; Serves 16

Ingredients:

- 5 cup blueberries, pureed
- 1 cup sugar
- 2 tsp ground cinnamon
- 1 medium lemon, zested and juiced

Instructions:

1. Place all ingredients in a 6-quart slow cooker and mix well.

2. Cover and cook on LOW for 1 hour.

3. Use a heat-safe kitchen utensil such as a wooden spoon to prop the lid slightly open while you continue to cook for a further 4-5 hours, stirring every hour.

4. The blueberry butter is ready when it has thickened and coats the back of a spoon.

5. The sauce can be stored in a refrigerator for up to 2 weeks in an airtight container and can also be frozen.

.Nutrition Facts Per Serving:

Calories 102, Fat 0g, Carbs 27g, Protein 1g, Fiber 2g, Potassium 64mg, Sodium 1mg

Low Sodium Beef Broth

Prep time: 20 minutes, cook time: 8 hours; Serves 10

Ingredients:

- 3lb soup bones
- 1lb beef shank
- 4 large carrots, peeled and cut into 1-inch chunks
- 2 medium onions, peeled and chopped
- 2 tbsp olive oil
- 2 bay leaves
- 5 garlic cloves, peeled and crushed
- 5 peppercorns
- 8 cup water

Instructions:

1. Preheat oven to 400°F.

2. Place the bones, beef shank, and vegetables in a large roasting pan drizzled with the oil and roast for 2 hours until brown.

3. Place the beef, bones, and vegetables into a 5 or a 6-quart slow cooker along with the bay, garlic, and peppercorns.

4. Use 1 cup of water to scrape up the meat juices and add to the slow cooker with the remaining water.

5. Cover and cook on LOW for 8 hours.

6. Chill the broth overnight, then strain well to remove all the solidified fat.

7. The strained broth is flavorsome and the perfect base for countless dishes yet is virtually calorie and sodium-free. The broth can be refrigerated or frozen.

Nutrition Facts Per Serving:

Calories 20, Fat <1g, Carbs 0g, Protein 3g, Fiber 0g, Potassium 206mg, Sodium 20mg

Prep time: 20 minutes, cook time: 4 hours; Serves 8

Ingredients:

- 1lb lean ground beef
- 2 cup low-sodium tomato sauce
- ½ cup water
- 1½ tbsp low-sodium Worcestershire sauce
- ¼ cup onion, finely chopped
- 1 tbsp ground mustard
- ½ tsp garlic powder
- ½ tsp freshly ground black pepper
- ½ tsp chili powder
- ¼ tsp cayenne pepper

Instructions:

1. Brown the ground beef in a large heavy-based frying pan.

2. Add the cooked ground beef along with all other ingredients to a 4 to 6- quart slow cooker.

3. Cover and cook on LOW for 4 hours.

4. Serve as a topping with low-sodium hot dogs.

Nutrition Facts Per Serving:

Calories 112, Fat 4g, Carbs 5g, Protein 12g, Fiber 1g, Potassium 210mg, Sodium 83mg

Prep time: 10 minutes, cook time: 5-6 hours; Serves 10

Ingredients:

- 12oz cranberries
- ½ cup orange juice
- 1 large cinnamon stick
- ½ cup honey

Instructions:

1. Place all the ingredients into a 2 or a 3-quart slow cooker and mix well.

2. Cook for 5-6 hours on LOW, or until the berries are soft and have dissolved down.

3. Remove the lid and continue to cook for 1-2 hours on HIGH until the sauce has thickened.

4. The sauce can be stored in a refrigerator for up to 2 weeks in an airtight container and can also be frozen.

Nutrition Facts Per Serving:

Calories 73, Fat 0g, Carbs 19g, Protein 0g, Fiber 2g, Potassium 65mg, Sodium 1mg

Chapter 4 Soups, Stews, and Chilis

Creamy Potato Soup

Prep time:15 minutes, cook time: 4 hours; Serves 8

Ingredients:

- Soup Ingredients
- 5 cup potatoes, peeled and diced
- 2 cup cauliflower, diced
- 2/3 cup celery, diced
- 1 cup onion, diced
- 6–8 cloves garlic, minced
- 4 cup sodium-free chicken broth (see recipe)
- ½ tsp dried thyme
- ¼ tsp dried cilantro
- Roux Ingredients
- 1 tbsp butter
- ¼ cup all-purpose flour
- 1 1/3 cup skim milk
- ¼ tsp black pepper
- ½ tsp low sodium salt

Instructions:

1. Place all soup ingredients in a 5 to 6-quart slow cooker.

2. Cook on HIGH for 4 hours.

3. Puree the soup with a blender.

4. Make a roux by melting the butter and adding the flour in a small heavy-based pan.

5. Cook for 3 to 4 minutes.

6. Gradually add the milk until you have a thickened sauce.

7. Season the sauce, then stir into the soup and heat through before serving.

Nutrition Facts Per Serving:

Calories 396, Fat 18g, Cholesterol 61mg, Carbs 7g, Protein 20g, Fiber 2g, Potassium 1222mg, Sodium 420mg

Creamy Cauliflower & Butternut Squash Soup

Prep time: 5 minutes, cook time: 2 hours; Serves 6

Ingredients:

- 1 onion, diced
- 1-2 tsp oil for sautéing
- 2-3 cloves garlic, minced
- 7 cup cauliflower florets
- 2 cup butternut squash, cubed
- 2 cup sodium-free vegetable or chicken broth (see recipe)
- 1 tsp paprika
- 1 tsp dried thyme
- ½ tsp red pepper flakes
- ¼ tsp low sodium salt
- ½ cup half and half

Instructions:

1. Sauté onion and garlic in a heavy-based skillet.

2. Place in a 5 to 6-quart with all other ingredients except the half and half.

3. Cook on HIGH for 4 hours.

4. Puree the soup in a blender.

5. Stir in the half and half, heat through and serve.

Nutrition Facts Per Serving:

Calories 100, Fat 2g, Carbs 16g, Protein 3g, Fiber 6g, Potassium 553mg, Sodium 345mg

Prep time:15 minutes, cook time: 4 hours; Serves 8

Ingredients:

- 4 cup sweet potatoes, peeled and chopped
- 2– 2 ½ cup broth
- 1lb lean ground turkey
- 14 oz diced low-sodium canned tomatoes
- 1 cup onion, chopped
- 2 –3 cup cauliflower, finely chopped
- 1 tsp garlic, minced
- 2 chipotles, chopped
- 1 tsp cumin
- ½ tsp paprika
- ½ tsp chili powder
- ¼ tsp black pepper
- ½ tsp low-sodium salt
- ½ cup bell peppers, chopped

Instructions:

1. Par-cook the potatoes until tender and place in a 4 to 6-quart slow cooker.

2. Brown meat in a skillet, then add to slow cooker.

3. Add all remaining ingredients to slow cooker and mix well.

4. Cover and cook on HIGH for 3-4 hrs.

5. Check the seasoning and garnish with fresh cilantro and finely chopped jalapenos.

Nutrition Facts Per Serving:

Calories 311, Fat 12g, Carbs 21g, Protein 19g, Fiber 2g, Potassium 565mg, Sodium 211mg

Prep time: 5 minutes, cook time: 6-8 hours; Serves 6

Ingredients:

- 1 cup pearl barley, uncooked
- 1lb lean beef stew meat, cut into 1-inch cubes
- 2 tbsp all-purpose white flour
- ¼ tsp black pepper
- ½ tsp low-sodium salt
- 2 tbsp canola oil
- ½ cup onion
- 1 large stalk celery, diced
- 1 garlic clove, minced
- 2 medium carrots, diced
- 2 bay leaves
- 2 quarts water
- 1 tsp salt-free Mrs. Dash® onion herb seasoning

Instructions:

1. Soak barley in 2 cups of water for 1 hour. Place in a 4-quart slow cooker.

2. Dust the meat in the black pepper and flour.

3. Heat the oil in a skillet and brown the meat. Add to the slow cooker.

4. Sauté the vegetables and garlic for a few minutes and add to the slow cooker.

5. Add the water and seasoning.

6. Cover and cook on LOW for 6-8 hours.

Nutrition Facts Per Serving:

Calories 246, Fat 8g, Carbs 21g, Protein 22g, Fiber 6g, Potassium 369mg, Sodium 150mg

Prep time: 30minutes, cook time: 6-8 hours; Serves 8

Ingredients:

- 2-3 large boneless skinless chicken breasts
- 2 15.5oz cans of reduced-sodium great northern beans, drained and rinsed
- 1 15oz of sweet golden corn, drained well and rinsed
- 1 4.5oz can green chilies, chopped
- 4 cup chicken broth (see recipe)
- 1 medium sweet yellow onion, chopped
- 3 garlic cloves, minced
- 1 lime, juiced
- 1 tsp cumin
- ½ tsp onion powder
- ½ tsp garlic powder
- 1 ½ tsp chili powder
- ¼ tsp cayenne pepper
- 1 tsp black pepper
- 1 tsp paprika

Instructions:

1. Place chicken breasts, beans, corn, green chilies, chopped onion, minced garlic, and spices into a 4 to 6-quart slow cooker.

2. Add chicken broth and squeeze the juice of one lime over the mixture.

3. Cook on LOW for 6 to 8 hours.

4. Before removing from the slow cooker, shred the chicken with forks.

Nutrition Facts Per Serving:

Calories 300, Fat 2g, Carbs 30g, Protein 32g, Fiber 6g, Potassium 549mg, Sodium 324mg

Prep time: 20 minutes, cook time: 10 hours; Serves 6

Ingredients:

- ½ cup all-purpose flour
- 1 tbsp garlic powder
- 1 tsp black pepper
- 1lb lean boneless pork chops, cut into 1-inch cubes
- 1 tbsp olive oil
- 1 8oz can of green chili peppers, drained well and chopped
- 1 garlic clove, minced
- 2 cup chicken broth (see recipe)
- 6 flour tortillas, burrito size
- ¾ cup iceberg lettuce, shredded
- ¼ cup cilantro, finely chopped
- 6 tbsp sour cream

Instructions:

1. Place the flour, garlic powder, and black pepper into a Ziploc bag.

2. Add the pork and coat well.

3. Heat the oil in a skillet and brown the pork.

4. Add the pork to a 4-quart slow cooker along with the broth, peppers, and garlic.

5. Cover and cook for 10 hours on LOW.

6. Place lettuce on a tortilla, top with stew and roll up burrito style.

7. Top with sour cream and cilantro.

Nutrition Facts Per Serving:

Calories 420, Fat 16g, Carbs 44g, Protein 25g, Fiber 3g, Potassium 454mg, Sodium 352mg

Turkey, Wild Rice, and Mushroom Soup

Prep time: 15 minutes, cook time: 2-3 hours; Serves 6

Ingredients:

- ½ cup onion, chopped
- ½ cup red bell pepper, chopped
- ½ cup carrots, chopped
- 2 garlic cloves, minced
- 2 cup cooked turkey, shredded
- 5 cup chicken broth (see recipe)
- ½ cup quick-cooking wild rice, uncooked
- 1 tbsp olive oil
- 1 cup mushrooms, sliced
- 2 bay leaves
- ¼ tsp Mrs. Dash® Original salt-free herb seasoning blend
- 1 tsp dried thyme
- ½ tsp low sodium salt
- ¼ tsp black pepper

Instructions:

1. Cook rice in a saucepan with 1-2 cups of broth. Set aside.

2. Heat oil in a skillet and sauté the onion, bell pepper, carrots, and garlic until soft. Add to a 4 to 6-quart slow cooker.

3. Add remaining ingredients to the slow cooker except for the rice and mushrooms.

4. Cover and cook for 2-3 hours on LOW.

5. Add the mushrooms and rice and cook for a further 15 minutes.

6. Remove the bay leaves and serve.

Nutrition Facts Per Serving:

Calories 210, Fat 2g, Carbs 15g, Protein 23g, Fiber 2g, Potassium 380mg, Sodium 115mg

Veggie Soup

Prep time: 20 minutes, cook time: 6 hours; Serves 6

Ingredients:

- 1 14oz no salt added diced tomatoes
- 1 large onion, diced
- 4 garlic cloves, minced
- 2 large carrots, diced
- 2 celery stalks, diced
- 1 medium parsnip, diced
- 1 large red bell pepper, diced
- 6 cup low sodium vegetable or chicken broth (see recipe)
- 3 cup cabbage, chopped
- ½ tsp low sodium salt
- ½ tsp black pepper
- 1 large sweet potato, peeled and diced

Instructions:

1. Place all ingredients in a slow cooker.

2. Cook for 4-6 hours on HIGH.

3. Serve the soup chunky or puree if desired.

Nutrition Facts Per Serving:

Calories 135, Fat 1g, Carbs 30g, Protein 4g, Fiber 7g, Potassium 880mg, Sodium 250mg

Chapter 5 Beans and Grains

Slow Cooker Lentil & Vegetable Casserole

Prep time: 15 minutes, cook time: 8-10 hours; Serves 8

Ingredients:

- 1 cup whole kernel corn
- 1 large red potato, cut into 1-inch cubes
- 4 carrots, sliced
- ½ cup onion, diced
- 2 stalks celery, sliced into ½-inch pieces
- 1 cup green beans, broken into 1-inch pieces
- ½ tsp paprika
- ½ tsp black pepper
- Low-sodium salt to taste
- 1 ½ cup low sodium tomato juice
- 3 cup low sodium vegetable or chicken broth (see recipe)
- 1 cup lentils

Instructions:

1. Add all of the ingredients, except lentils, to a 4 to a 6-quart slow cooker and stir well.

2. Cook on LOW for 8 to 10 hours.

3. Add the lentils during the final hour of cooking time.

Nutrition Facts Per Serving:

Calories 221, Fat 12g, Carbs 42g, Protein 11g, Fiber 11g, Potassium 427mg, Sodium 312mg

Prep time: 5 minutes, cook time: 4 hours; Serves 4

Ingredients:

- 1 15oz can of chickpeas, drained and rinsed well
- 1 tbsp olive oil
- ¼ tsp low-sodium salt

Instructions:

1. Place the chickpeas on kitchen paper to remove excess moisture.

2. Put the chickpeas, oil, and salt in a Ziploc bag and shake well.

3. Place the chickpeas into a 5-quart or larger slow cooker and cover.

4. Cook on HIGH for 4 hours, stirring every 30 minutes.

5. Spread the chickpeas on a baking sheet and allow to cool before storing in an airtight container.

Nutrition Facts Per Serving:

Calories 160, Fat 5g, Carbs 24g, Protein 5g, Fiber 4g, Potassium 184mg, Sodium 415mg

Basic Beans

Prep time: 5 minutes, cook time: 8-10 hours; Serves 8

Ingredients:

- 1lb dried beans, such as pinto beans, black beans or kidney beans
- Water
- 1 garlic clove, minced
- ¼ tsp low-sodium salt
- ¼ tsp freshly ground black pepper

Instructions:

1. Place the beans, salt, and garlic in a 5-quart or larger slow cooker.

2. Add enough water to cover the beans by about 3 inches.

3. Cover and cook on LOW for 8 to 10 hours.

4. Can be refrigerated or frozen. Heat through in a saucepan to reheat.

Nutrition Facts Per Serving:

Calories 163, Fat 0g, Carbs 36g, Protein 7g, Fiber 8g, Potassium 783mg, Sodium 43mg

Prep time: 15 minutes, cook time: 6-8 hours; Serves 8

Ingredients:

- 1 tbsp olive oil
- 1 cup onion, diced
- ¾ cup red bell pepper, diced
- 1 stalk celery, diced
- 2 cloves garlic, minced
- 1 tsp low-sodium sea salt to taste
- ¼ tsp cayenne pepper
- ½ tsp freshly ground black pepper
- 2 tsp fresh thyme
- 1 bay leaf
- 2 15oz can dark red kidney beans
- 3 cup low-sodium chicken broth (see recipe)
- 2 cup uncooked long-grain brown rice

Instructions:

1. Heat the oil in a skillet, heat olive oil and fry onions, bell pepper, garlic, and celery, until tender.

2. Add to a 4-6-quart slow cooker and cook on LOW for 6-8 hours.

3. Cook the rice separately and add to the beans at the end of cooking.

4. Remove the bay leaves before serving. Ideal served with low-sodium meatballs.

Nutrition Facts Per Serving:

Calories 171, Fat 2g, Carbs 38g, Protein 15g, Fiber 4g, Potassium 817mg, Sodium 200mg

Slow Cooker Butternut Squash & Parmesan Risotto

Prep time: 15 minutes, cook time: 4-5 hours; Serves 8

Ingredients:

- 1¼ cup risotto rice
- 2 tbsp olive oil
- 3½ cup vegetable or chicken broth (see recipe)
- 2 cup butternut squash, cubed
- 1 small onion, diced
- 2 cloves garlic, minced
- 1 tsp dried rubbed sage
- ¼ cup non-fat low-sodium parmesan cheese, grated

Instructions:

1. Place all ingredients, except the butternut squash and parmesan, in a 4 to 6-quart slow cooker.

2. Cook on LOW for 4 to 5 hours.

3. Add the butternut squash during the final hour of cooking.

4. Cook until the rice is tender and all the liquid has been absorbed.

4. Stir in the parmesan cheese before serving.

5. An ideal vegetarian dish or serve as a side dish with meat, fish or poultry.

Nutrition Facts Per Serving:

Calories 177, Fat 5g, Carbs 30g, Protein 4g, Fiber 2g, Potassium 349mg, Sodium 69mg

Prep time: 20 minutes, cook time: 2-3 hours; Serves 6

Ingredients:

- 1 24oz jar low-sodium spaghetti sauce
- 8oz uncooked whole-wheat spaghetti
- 1 cup low fat cottage cheese
- 1 cup skim mozzarella cheese, shredded
- 1 cup low-fat ricotta cheese
- 1 tsp dried oregano
- 1 tbsp chopped (fresh) basil or 1 teaspoon dried basil
- Low sodium salt to taste
- ½ tsp ground black pepper

Instructions:

1. Add all the ingredients to a 4to 6-quart slow cooker.

2. Cook on LOW for 2-3 hours until the pasta is cooked al dente.

3. Serve sprinkled with low sodium parmesan as a vegetarian dish or serve with low-sodium meatballs.

Nutrition Facts Per Serving:

Calories 289, Fat 9g, Carbs 38g, Protein 15g, Fiber 6g, Potassium 565mg, Sodium 142mg

Prep time: 10 minutes, cook time: 8-10 hours; Serves 8

Ingredients:

- 2 cup wild rice blend
- 1 tbsp olive oil
- 4 cup vegetable broth
- ¾ cup shallots, finely chopped
- 2 cup sliced mushrooms
- 1 clove garlic, minced
- 1 tbsp fresh rosemary
- 1 tbsp fresh sage
- 1 tsp fresh thyme

Instructions:

1. Place the rice and oil into a 4 to 6-quart slow cooker and stir well to coat the rice grains.

2. Add the remaining ingredients and cover.

3. Cook on LOW for 5 hours or until the rice is tender.

Nutrition Facts Per Serving:

Calories 156, Fat 2g, Carbs 27g, Protein 8g, Fiber 2g, Potassium 312mg, Sodium 310mg

Chapter 6 Snacks

Chocolate & Banana Bread

Prep time:15 minutes, cook time: 2 hours; Serves 16

Ingredients:

- 1 box yellow cake mix
- 3 large eggs
- 1/3 cup vegetable oil
- 5 medium bananas ripe, mashed
- 1 ½ cup semi-sweet chocolate chips
- ½ cup chopped pecans, optional
- Non-stick spray

Instructions:

1. Mix all the ingredients well in a large mixing bowl. You can use a spoon or mixer.

2. Spray a 6 quart or larger slow cooker with non-stick spray.

3. Pour in cake batter and cover.

4. Cover and cook on HIGH for 2 to 3 hours.

5. The banana bread is cooked when golden brown and a skewer inserted into the bread comes out clean.

Nutrition Facts Per Serving:

Calories 374, Fat 18g, Carbs 50g, Protein 3g, Fiber 1g, Potassium 147mg, Sodium 222mg

Prep time: 5minutes, cook time: 3 hours; Serves 24

Ingredients:

- 24oz cream cheese, cubed
- 1lb lump crab meat or imitation crab meat
- ½ cup milk
- ½ cup green onions, chopped
- 1 ½ tbsp low-sodium Worcestershire Sauce
- 1 tbsp horseradish

Instructions:

1. Place all the ingredients into a 3-quart slow cooker and mix well.

2. Cover and cook on LOW for 3 hours, stirring occasionally.

3. The dip is cooked when the cheese has melted thoroughly into the dip.

4. Turn the slow cooker to WARM and serve the dip with low-sodium chips or crackers.

Nutrition Facts Per Serving:

Calories 119, Fat 9g, Carbs 3g, Protein 6g, Fiber 0g, Potassium 21mg, Sodium 186mg

Prep time: 15 minutes, cook time: 2 hours; Serves 16

Ingredients:

- 1lb walnuts
- ½ cup butter
- ½ cup maple syrup
- 1 tsp vanilla extract

Instructions:

1. Place all the ingredients into a 4-quart slow cooker.

2. Cook on LOW for 2 hours, stirring occasionally during cooking

3. Cool the walnuts on parchment paper before storing in an airtight container.

Nutrition Facts Per Serving:

Calories 264, Fat24g, Carbs 10g, Protein 4g, Fiber 2g, Potassium 127mg, Sodium 2mg

Ranch Mushrooms

Prep time: 5 minutes, cook time: 4 hours; Serves 4

Ingredients:

- 1lb mushrooms
- ½ cup trans-free margarine, melted
- 1 packet Salt-free Ranch Dressing Mix (such as Mrs. Dash)

Instructions:

1. Place the mushrooms to 3 to 4- quart slow cooker.

2. Blend the melted margarine with the dry ranch dressing mix and pour into the slow cooker.

3. Cover and cook on LOW for 4 hours.

Nutrition Facts Per Serving:

Calories 252, Fat 24g, Carbs 7g, Protein 4g, Fiber 1g, Potassium 367mg, Sodium 8mg

Prep time: 15 minutes, cook time: 4-6 hours; Serves 8

Ingredients:

- 1.5lb sodium-free turkey meatballs such as Jennie-O Brand
- ¼ cup brown sugar
- ¼ cup low-sodium hot sauce
- ¼ cup honey
- ¼ cup apricot preserve
- 2 tbsp low sodium soy sauce
- 1 ½ tbsp cornstarch

Instructions:

1. Add the defrosted meatballs to a 4 to 5-quart slow cooker.

2. Mix the remaining ingredients in a small bowl and pour the sauce into the slow cooker.

3. Cover and cook on LOW for 4 to 6 hours.

4. Turn the slow cooker to WARM and serve.

Nutrition Facts Per Serving:

Calories 264, Fat 13g, Carbs 24g, Protein 5g, Fiber 0g, Potassium 224mg, Sodium 30mg

Prep time: 10 minutes, cook time: 2-3 hours; Serves 8

Ingredients:

- 1 cup cream cheese, softened
- ½ cup roasted red peppers, drained
- 1 cup reduced-fat sour cream
- 4 tsp low-sodium hot pepper sauce
- 2 cup cooked, shredded chicken

Instructions:

1. Puree the red peppers in a mini blender.

2. Mix all the ingredients well and place in a 3-quart slow cooker.

3. Cover and cook for 2 to 3 hours on LOW, stirring occasionally.

4. Turn the slow cooker to WARM and serve with vegetable for dipping such as celery, carrots, lettuce, and cauliflower.

Nutrition Facts Per Serving:

Calories 146, Fat 10g, Carbs 4g, Protein 10g, Fiber 0g, Potassium 162mg, Sodium 132mg

Prep time: 15 minutes, cook time: 6 hours; Serves 8

Ingredients:

- 1lb skinless chicken breast
- ½ tsp garlic powder
- ¼ tsp black pepper
- 1 small onion, sliced
- 1 cup water
- 1/3 cup low-sodium barbeque sauce
- 8 mini whole wheat buns

Instructions:

1. Place the chicken breasts in a 3-quart slow cooker.

2. Sprinkle with the garlic powder and pepper.

3. Top with onion and pour in the water.

4. Cover and cook on LOW for 6 hours.

5. Drain the cooking water and shred the chicken.

6. Stir in the barbeque sauce and cook for 15 more minutes.

7. Make the sliders by topping the buns with the barbeque chicken sauce.

Nutrition Facts Per Serving:

Calories 180, Fat 4g, Carbs 22g, Protein 16g, Fiber 3g, Potassium 230mg, Sodium 240mg

Chapter 7 Desserts

Chocolate Chip Pan Cookies

Prep time:20 minutes, cook time: 2 hours; Serves 24

Ingredients:

- 1 cup butter, softened
- 2 whole eggs, beaten
- ½ cup brown sugar
- ½ cup granulated sugar
- 1 tbsp vanilla extract
- 2 cup all-purpose flour
- ½ tsp baking soda
- 1 cup semi-sweet chocolate chips
- ¼ tsp low-sodium salt

Instructions:

1. In a bowl, mix all the ingredients except the chocolate chips.

2. Stir in the chocolate chips then spread the dough along the base and sides of a 6-quart or larger slow cooker covered in aluminum foil.

3. Cook on HIGH for 2 to 2.5 hours.

4. Remove the foil and cookies from the slow cooker and cut into pieces.

Nutrition Facts Per Serving:

Calories 231, Fat 11g, Carbs 17g, Protein 3g, Fiber 1g, Potassium 52mg, Sodium 41mg

Chocolate Bread Pudding

Prep time: 10 minutes, cook time: 2.5-3 hours; Serves 6

Ingredients:

- 12 slices low-sodium white bread, cubed
- ½ cup raisins
- ½ cup semi-sweet chocolate chips
- 4 large eggs, beaten
- 1 ¾ cup milk
- ½ cup granulated sugar
- 1/3 cup unsweetened cocoa powder
- 1 tsp vanilla extract
- Non-stick spray

Instructions:

1. Spray the base of a 5 quart or larger slow cooker with non-stick cooking spray.

2. Add bread cubes, raisins and chocolate chips to the slow cooker.

3. Whisk together the eggs, milk, sugar, cocoa powder, and vanilla extract and pour into a 5-quart or larger slow cooker.

4. Cover and cook on LOW for 2.5 to 3 hours.

Nutrition Facts Per Serving:

Calories 461, Fat 12g, Carbs 84g, Protein 13g, Fiber 6g, Potassium 508mg, Sodium 112mg

Pineapple Dump Cake

Prep time: 5 minutes, cook time: 2-3 hours; Serves 12

Ingredients:

- 14oz canned crushed pineapple
- 1 tbsp granulated sugar
- 1 box yellow cake mix
- 1 cup margarine, melted

Instructions:

1. Arrange the pineapple on the base of a 5 quart or larger slow cooker.

2. Sprinkle the sugar and dry cake mix on top of the pineapple.

4. Pour over the melted margarine and cover.

5. Cook on HIGH for 2 to 3 hours.

Nutrition Facts Per Serving:

Calories 328, Fat 17g, Carbs 42g, Protein 1g, Fiber 0g, Potassium 66mg, Sodium 282mg

Crock-Pot Zucchini Cake with Cream Cheese Frosting

Prep time: 30minutes, cook time: 2-3 hours; Serves 24

Ingredients:

- 2 cup all-purpose flour
- 2 tsp ground cinnamon
- 2 tsp baking soda
- 1 tsp low-sodium salt
- ½ tsp ground nutmeg
- ¼ tsp baking powder
- 3 large eggs
- 2 cup sugar
- ½ cup vegetable oil
- ½ cup unsweetened apple sauce
- 2 tsp vanilla extract
- 1 tsp lemon zest
- 2 cup unpeeled zucchini, grated & excess moisture removed
- 1 cup pecans or walnuts, chopped
- ½ cup raisins
- Cream Cheese Frosting
- 1½ cup cream cheese, softened
- 2 cup powdered sugar
- 1 tsp freshly squeezed lemon juice
- ½ tsp vanilla extract

Instructions:

1. Spray a 4-quart slow cooker with non-stick cooking spray.

2. Mix the dry ingredients in a large mixing bowl and set aside.

3. Mix the eggs, sugar, vegetable oil, apple sauce, lemon zest, and vanilla extract and add to the dry ingredients.

4. Stir in zucchini, pecans, and raisins.

5. Pour batter into a 5-quart or larger slow cooker and cook on HIGH for 2 to 3 hours.

6. Check that the cake is cooked with a skewer.

7. Leave to cool before topping with frosting.

8. To make the frosting, cream the frosting ingredients with a mixer for 3 minutes and spread over the cooled cake when light and fluffy.

Nutrition Facts Per Serving:

Calories 393, Fat 15g, Carbs 62g, Protein 6g, Fiber 3g, Potassium 122mg, Sodium 187mg

Raspberry Almond Coffee Cake Recipe

Prep time: 20 minutes, cook time: 2-3 hours; Serves 12

Ingredients

Coffee Cake

- 3 cups all-purpose flour
- 1 cup sugar
- ½ cup unsalted butter, cubed
- 1 tsp baking soda
- 1 tsp baking powder
- 2 large eggs
- 1½ cup fat-free Greek yogurt
- ½ cup unsweetened apple sauce
- 1 tsp vanilla extract
- 1 tsp almond extract
- 4 cup fresh raspberries
- 4oz toasted sliced almonds

Icing

- ½ cup powdered sugar
- 2 tbsp fat-free milk
- ¼ tsp vanilla extract
- ¼ tsp almond extract

Instructions:

1. Spray the base of 6-quart or larger slow cooker.

2. Mix cake ingredients well until you have a stiff batter.

3. Spoon batter into a slow cooker and cook on HIGH for 2 to 3 hours.

4. When the cake is cool, top with icing.

5. To make the icing simply blend icing ingredients well in a small bowl.

Nutrition Facts Per Serving:

Calories 513, Fat 14g, Carbs 86g, Protein 14g, Fiber 9g, Potassium 249mg, Sodium 108mg

Prep time: 20 minutes, cook time: 6 hours; Serves 6

Ingredients:

- 3lbs apples Granny Smith, washed, cored, and sliced
- ½ cup granulated sugar
- ½ cup brown sugar
- 1 tsp ground cinnamon
- ½ tsp ground nutmeg
- 2 tbsp butter, cut into slices

Instructions:

1. Layer the base of a 6-quart slow cooker with the apples.

2. Mix the sugar, brown sugar, nutmeg, cinnamon and butter, and sprinkle over the apples.

3. Cover with the lid slightly ajar on LOW for 6 hours. Stir once midway through cooking.

Nutrition Facts Per Serving:

Calories 310, Fat 1g, Carbs 45g, Protein 1g, Fiber 6g, Potassium 311mg, Sodium 8mg

Rhubarb & Strawberry Crisp

Prep time: 10 minutes, cook time: 2-3 hours; Serves 6

Ingredients:

- 1/3 cup sugar
- ½ tsp ground cinnamon
- 3 cup rhubarb, chopped
- 1 cup strawberries, sliced
- 2/3 cup quick-cooking oats
- 2/3 cup brown sugar
- ½ cup all-purpose flour
- 4 tbsp butter, softened
- 1 tsp baking powder
- 1/8 tsp low sodium salt

Instructions:

1. Arrange the rhubarb and strawberries in a 5-quart or larger slow cooker.

2. Sprinkle with cinnamon and sugar.

3. Mix the remaining ingredients to form a crumb and use to top the fruit.

4. Cover and cook on HIGH for 2 - 3 hours.

Nutrition Facts Per Serving:

Calories 426, Fat 10g, Carbs 80g, Protein 8g, Fiber 6g, Potassium 613mg, Sodium 73mg

Chapter 8 Fish and Seafood

Sweet and Sour Shrimp

Prep time: 10 minutes, cook time: 5.5 hours; Serves 3-4

Ingredients:

- 1 cup Chinese pea pods, thawed
- 1 14oz can pineapple chunks
- 2 tablespoons cornstarch
- 3 tbsp sugar
- 1 cup chicken stock (see recipe)
- ½ cup reserved pineapple juice
- 1 tbsp low-sodium soy sauce
- ½ tsp ground ginger
- 1lb large cooked shrimp
- 2 tbsp cider vinegar
- 1 cup of rice, cooked

Instructions:

1. Place the pea pods and pineapple in a 4 to 6-quart slow cooker.

2. Blend the cornstarch and sugar with the chicken stock and pineapple juice and heat in a small saucepan until thickened.

3. Pour the sauce into the slow cooker and add the ginger and soy sauce.

4. Cover and cook on LOW for 3 to 4 hours.

5. Add the shrimp and vinegar and cook for a further 15 minutes.

6. Serve with the hot cooked rice.

Nutrition Facts Per Serving:

Calories 395, Fat 2g, Carbs 61g, Protein 33g, Fiber 5g, Potassium 796mg, Sodium 215 mg

Prep time: 20 minutes, cook time: 6 hours; Serves 6

Ingredients:

- 1lb salmon fillet, cut into small fillets
- 1 tbsp extra-virgin olive oil
- ½ large onion, thinly sliced
- ¼ tsp ground ginger
- ¼ tsp dried dill
- ¼ tsp low-sodium salt
- ¼ tsp black pepper
- ½ lemon, thinly sliced

Instructions:

1. Arrange the onions in the base of a 4 to 6-quart slow cooker.

2. Place each piece of salmon in an aluminum foil packet and sprinkle with spices and top with lemon slices.

3. Place the salmon packets on top of the onions in the slow cooker and cover.

4. Cook on LOW for 6 to 8 hours.

5. Serve the salmon on top of the onions.

Nutrition Facts Per Serving:

Calories 215, Fat 11g, Carbs 7g, Protein 24g, Fiber 2g, Potassium 520mg, Sodium 200mg

Prep time: 15 minutes, cook time: 4 hours; Serves 4

Ingredients:

- 1 14oz can of no-added sodium crushed tomatoes
- 1 6oz can of no-added salt tomato paste
- 1 garlic clove, minced
- 1 tsp low-sodium salt
- 2 tsp fresh basil, chopped
- ½ tsp dried oregano
- ¼ tsp freshly ground black pepper
- ½ tsp crushed red pepper flakes
- 2 tbsp fresh parsley, minced
- 1lb cooked shrimp, peeled and deveined
- ½ cup low-sodium Parmesan cheese, grated
- 4 cup cooked spaghetti

Instructions:

1. Place the tomatoes, tomato paste, garlic, salt, basil, oregano, salt, black pepper, and crushed red pepper, into a 4 to 6-quart slow cooker. if using.

2. Cover and cook on LOW for 4 to 5 hours.

3. Add the shrimp and parsley and cook on HIGH for 10 minutes.

4. Serve the shrimp on top of the hot cooked pasta with low-sodium Parmesan cheese.

Nutrition Facts Per Serving:

Calories 509, Fat 5g, Carbs 69g, Protein 48g, Fiber 7g, Potassium 629mg, Sodium 400mg

Prep time: 20 minutes, cook time: 6-8 hours; Serves 8

Ingredients:

- 1 fillet of seabass, cod or other white fish, cubed
- 1 dozen each large shrimp, scallops, mussels & clams
- 1 28 ounces no-added salt crushed tomatoes with juice
- 1 8oz no-added salt tomato sauce
- ½ cup onion, chopped
- 1 cup dry white wine
- 1/3 cup olive oil
- 3 garlic cloves, minced
- ½ cup parsley, chopped
- 1 green pepper, chopped
- 1 hot pepper, chopped
- ½ tsp low sodium salt
- 1 tsp thyme
- 2 tsp basil
- 1 tsp oregano
- ½ tsp paprika
- ½ tsp cayenne pepper

Instructions:

1. Place all ingredients except seafood in a 4 to 6-quart slow cooker and cover.

2. Cook on LOW for 6 to 8 hours.

3. Add the fish about 30 minutes towards the end of the cooking time and turn up the heat to HIGH.

Nutrition Facts Per Serving:

Calories 434, Fat 16g, Carbs 27g, Protein 39g, Fiber 4g, Potassium 714mg, Sodium 378mg

Prep time: 15 minutes, cook time: 6 hours; Serves 6

Ingredients:

- 2lb white fish fillets, cut into 1-inch pieces
- ¼lb low-sodium bacon, diced
- 1 medium onion, chopped
- 4 medium red-skinned potatoes, peeled and cubed
- 2 cup water
- 1 low sodium salt
- ¼ tsp black pepper
- 1 12oz can evaporated milk

Instructions:

1. Fry the bacon in a skillet for a few minutes with the onion.

2. Add the bacon to the slow cooker with the remaining ingredients except for the evaporated milk.

3. Cover and cook on HIGH for 5 to 6 hours.

4. Add the milk during the last hour of cooking.

Nutrition Facts Per Serving:

Calories 311, Fat 13g, Carbs 27g, Protein 14g, Fiber 12g, Potassium 911mg, Sodium 600mg

Prep time: 15 minutes, cook time: 4 hours; Serves 2-3

Ingredients:

- 1½ cup celery, diced
- 1¼ cup onion, chopped
- 1 cup bell pepper, chopped
- 1 8oz can no-added salt tomato sauce
- 1 28oz no-added salt can whole tomatoes
- 1 garlic clove, minced
- ½ tsp low-sodium salt
- ½ tsp salt-free Creole seasoning
- ¼ tsp freshly ground black pepper
- 6 drops Tabasco sauce
- 1lb shrimp, deveined and shelled

Instructions:

1. Place all the ingredients into a 3-quart slow cooker except the shrimp.

2. Cook 3 to 4 hours on high or 6 to 8 hours on low.

3. Add shrimp during last 30 minutes of cooking.

4. Serve over hot cooked rice

Nutrition Facts Per Serving:

Calories 388, Fat 3g, Carbs 42g, Protein 52g, Fiber 8g, Potassium 874mg, Sodium 600mg

Chapter 9 Poultry & Meat

Creamy Mushroom and Broccoli Chicken

Prep time:15 minutes, cook time: 6 hours; Serves 6

Ingredients:

- 1 10.5oz can of low-sodium cream of mushroom soup
- 1 21oz can of low-sodium cream of Chicken Soup
- 2 whole cooked chicken breasts, chopped or shredded
- 2 cup milk
- 1lb broccoli florets
- ¼ tsp garlic powder

Instructions:

1. Place all ingredients to a 5 quart or larger slow cooker and mix well.

2. Cover and cook on LOW for 6 hours.

3. Serve with potatoes, pasta, or rice.

Nutrition Facts Per Serving:

Calories 155, Fat 2g, Carbs 19g, Protein 12g, Fiber 2g, Potassium 755mg, Sodium 35mg

Prep time: 10 minutes, cook time: 4 hours; Serves 4

Ingredients:

- 1lb skinless chicken breasts
- 1 medium onion, thinly sliced
- 1 15 oz can chickpeas, drained and rinsed well
- 2 medium sweet potatoes, peeled and diced
- ½ cup light coconut milk
- ½ cup chicken stock (see recipe)
- 1 15oz can sodium-free tomato sauce
- 2 tbsp curry powder
- 1 tsp low-sodium salt
- ½ cayenne powder
- 1 cup green peas
- 2 tbsp lemon juice

Instructions:

1. Place the chicken breasts, onion, chickpeas, and sweet potatoes into a 4 to 6-quart slow cooker.

2. Mix the coconut milk, chicken stock, tomato sauce, curry powder, salt, and cayenne together and pour into the slow cooker, stirring to coat well.

3. Cover and cook on Low for 8 hours or High for 4 hours.

4. Stir in the peas and lemon juice 5 minutes before serving.

Nutrition Facts Per Serving:

Calories 302, Fat 5g, Carbs 43g, Protein 24g, Fiber 9g, Potassium 573mg, Sodium 800mg

Prep time:20 minutes, cook time: 6 hours; Serves 6

Ingredients:

- 1 2-3lb boneless pork loin roast
- ½ tsp low-sodium salt
- ¼ tsp pepper
- 1 tbsp canola oil
- 3 medium apples, peeled and sliced
- ¼ cup honey
- 1 small red onion, halved and sliced
- 1 tbsp ground cinnamon

Instructions:

1. Season the pork with salt and pepper.

2. Heat the oil in a skillet and brown the pork on all sides.

3. Arrange half the apples in the base of a 4 to 6-quart slow cooker.

4. Top with the honey and remaining apples.

5. Sprinkle with cinnamon and cover.

6. Cover and cook on low for 6-8 hours until the meat is tender.

Nutrition Facts Per Serving:

Calories 290, Fat 10g, Carbs 19g, Protein 29g, Fiber 2g, Potassium 789mg, Sodium 22mg

Lemon & Herb Turkey Breasts

Prep time:25 minutes, cook time: 3 1/2 hours; Serves 12

Ingredients:

- 1 can (14-1/2 ounces) chicken broth
- 1/2 cup lemon juice
- 1/4 cup packed brown sugar
- 1/4 cup fresh sage
- 1/4 cup fresh thyme leaves
- 1/4 cup lime juice
- 1/4 cup cider vinegar
- 1/4 cup olive oil
- 1 envelope low-sodium onion soup mix
- 2 tbsp Dijon mustard
- 1 tbsp fresh marjoram, minced
- 1 tsp paprika
- 1 tsp garlic powder
- 1 tsp pepper
- ½ tsp low-sodium salt
- 2 2lb boneless skinless turkey breast halves

Instructions:

1. Make a marinade by blending all the ingredients in a blender.

2. Pour over the turkey and leave overnight.

3. Place the turkey and marinade in a 4 to 6-quart slow cooker and cover.

4. Cover and cook on HIGH for 3-1/2 to 4-1/2 hours or until a thermometer reads 165°.

Nutrition Facts Per Serving:

Calories 219, Fat 5g, Carbs 3g, Protein 36g, Fiber 0g, Potassium 576mg, Sodium 484mg

Beef Chimichangas

Prep time: 10minutes, cook time: 10-12 hours; Serves 16

Ingredients:

Shredded Beef

- 3lb boneless beef chuck roast, fat trimmed away
- 3 tbsp low-sodium Taco Seasoning Mix
- 1 10oz canned low-sodium diced tomatoes
- 6oz canned diced green chilies with the juice
- 3 garlic cloves, minced

To Serve

- 16 medium Flour Tortillas
- Sodium-free refried beans
- Mexican rice, sour cream, Cheddar cheese
- Guacamole, salsa, lettuce

Instructions:

1. Arrange the beef in a 5-quart or larger slow cooker.

2. Sprinkle over taco seasoning and coat well.

3. Add tomatoes and garlic and cover.

4. Cook on LOW for 10 to 12 hours.

5. When cooked remove the beef and shred.

6. Make burritos out of the shredded beef, refried beans, Mexican rice, and cheese.

7. Bake for 10 minutes at 350° F until brown.

8. Serve with salsa, lettuce, and guacamole.

Nutrition Facts Per Serving:

Calories 249, Fat 18g, Carbs 3g, Protein 33g, Fiber 5g, Potassium 633mg, Sodium 457mg

Prep time: 5minutes, cook time: 8 hours; Serves 6

Ingredients:

- 3lb beef short ribs
- ½ cup red wine
- 1 tbsp olive oil
- 3 garlic cloves, minced
- ¼ cup brown sugar
- Low-sodium salt and pepper to taste

Instructions:

1. Season ribs with salt and pepper.

2. Place ribs into a 5 quart or larger slow cooker.

3. Mix the red wine, olive oil, and garlic together and pour over ribs.

4. Cover and cook on LOW for 8 hours.

5. Remove the ribs and keep warm.

6. Transfer the juices to a small saucepan with the sugar and reduce by half to make a sauce to pour over the ribs.

Nutrition Facts Per Serving:

Calories 470, Fat 26g, Carbs 11g, Protein 43g, Fiber 0g, Potassium 613mg, Sodium 174mg

Prep time: 5 minutes, cook time: 5-6 hours; Serves 6

Ingredients:

- 2lb lean ground beef
- 2 whole eggs, beaten
- ¾ cup milk
- ¾ cup breadcrumbs
- ½ cup chicken broth (see recipe)
- ¼ cup onion, finely diced
- 3 garlic cloves, minced
- 1 tsp low-sodium salt
- ¼ tsp freshly ground black pepper
- ¼ cup low sodium chili sauce
- Non-stick spray

Instructions:

1. Mix the beaten eggs, milk, oatmeal, spices, onion, garlic, and chicken broth until well combined.

2. Mix in the beef and place in a 5-quart or larger slow cooker, sprayed with non-stick spray.

3. Cover and cook on LOW for 5 to 6 hours.

4. Serve with low-sodium ketchup.

Nutrition Facts Per Serving:

Calories 280, Fat 10g, Carbs 9g, Protein 37g, Fiber 1g, Potassium 648mg, Sodium 325mg

Crock-Pot Peachy Pork Chops

Prep time: 30minutes, cook time: 2-3 hours; Serves 8

Ingredients:

- 4 large peaches, pitted and peeled
- 1 onion, finely minced
- ¼ cup Ketchup
- ¼ cup low-sodium honey barbecue sauce
- 2 tbsp brown sugar
- 1 tbsp low sodium soy sauce
- ¼ tsp low-sodium garlic salt
- ½ tsp ground ginger
- 2lb boneless pork chops
- 3 tbsp olive oil

Instructions:

1. Puree the peaches with a blender.

2. Mix the peach puree with the onion, ketchup, barbecue sauce, brown sugar, soy sauce, salt, garlic salt, and ginger.

3. Brown the pork chops in a large skillet then transfer to a 6-quart or larger slow cooker.

4. Pour the sauce over the pork chops and cover.

5. Cook for 5 to 6 hours on HIGH.

Nutrition Facts Per Serving:

Calories 252, Fat 8g, Carbs 18g, Protein 26g, Fiber 1g, Potassium 710mg, Sodium 325mg

Chapter 10 Vegetable &Vegan

Green Beans with Bacon

Prep time: 30minutes, cook time: 6-8 hours; Serves 10

Ingredients:

- 12oz low-sodium bacon
- 29oz canned green beans
- 1 medium onion, chopped
- ½ cup maple syrup
- ¼ cup brown sugar

Instructions:

1. Fry bacon and onion in a skillet and transfer to a 5 quart or larger slow cooker.

2. Add remaining ingredients and stir well.

3. Cover and cook on LOW for 6 to 8 hours.

Nutrition Facts Per Serving:

Calories 185, Fat 9g, Carbs 17g, Protein 12g, Fiber 1g, Potassium 125mg, Sodium 445mg

Coconut & Pecan Sweet Potatoes

Prep time: 20 minutes, cook time: 4-5 hours; Serves 16

Ingredients:

- 4lb sweet potatoes, peeled and diced
- ½ cup pecans, chopped
- ½ cup unsweetened flaked coconut
- ½ cup butter, melted
- 1/3 cup sugar
- 1/3 cup brown sugar
- ½ tsp vanilla extract
- ¼ tsp low sodium salt

Instructions:

1. Place the sweet potatoes in a 5 quart or larger slow cooker.

2. Mix together the pecans, coconut, melted butter, both sugars, vanilla extract, and salt.

3. Toss the nut mixture with the sweet potatoes.

4. Cover and cook on LOW for 4 to 5 hours.

Nutrition Facts Per Serving:

Calories 307, Fat 16g, Carbs 42g, Protein 3g, Fiber 5g, Potassium 419mg, Sodium 50mg

Prep time: 20 minutes, cook time: 8-10 hours; Serves 32

Ingredients:

- 1 onion, diced
- 7 medium carrots, peeled & diced
- 2 green bell peppers, diced
- 3 small zucchinis, diced
- 2 cups mushrooms, roughly chopped
- 87oz canned crushed tomatoes
- 2 tbsp dried basil
- 1 tbsp dried oregano
- 1 tsp dried rosemary
- 1 whole bay leaf, crumbled
- 3 garlic cloves, minced

Instructions:

1. Place all ingredients into a 6-quart or larger slow cooker and mix well.

2. Cover and cook on LOW 8 to 10 hours.

Nutrition Facts Per Serving:

Calories 43, Fat <1g, Carbs 10g, Protein 2g, Fiber 3g, Potassium 411mg, Sodium 112mg

Bombay Potatoes

Prep time: 45 minutes, cook time: 4-6 hours; Serves 6

Ingredients:

- 3 tbsp olive oil
- 2 tsp mustard seeds
- 1 onion, peeled and diced
- 1 teaspoon Garam Masala Spice
- 1 tsp ground ginger
- 1 ½ tsp turmeric
- ½ tsp ground cumin
- ½ tsp chili powder
- ¼ tsp red chili flakes
- 3lb potatoes, peeled and diced into ½ inch cubes
- 14.5oz canned low-sodium diced tomatoes or fresh tomatoes
- 1 tsp low sodium salt
- ½ tsp freshly ground black pepper
- ¼ cup fresh cilantro, finely chopped

Instructions:

1. Cook the mustard seeds in a large skillet until they begin to pop.

2. Add the onions are spices and cook for a further 5 minutes.

3. Add the potatoes, tomatoes and onion mixture to a 6-quart slow cooker and cover.

4. Cook for 4 to 6 hours on LOW.

Nutrition Facts Per Serving:

Calories 280, Fat 8g, Carbs 10g, Protein 2g, Fiber 3g, Potassium 911mg, Sodium 78mg

Potato & Broccoli Gratin

Prep time: 20 minutes, cook time: 3-4 hours; Serves 6

Ingredients:

- 5 medium potatoes, sliced
- 2 cup broccoli florets, chopped
- ½ tsp freshly ground black pepper
- ½ tsp low sodium salt
- ¼ cup unsalted margarine
- ¼ cup all-purpose flour
- 1 medium onion, minced
- 1 garlic clove, minced
- 1 cup milk
- 1 cup low-sodium Cheddar cheese

Instructions:

1. Arrange the potato slices and broccoli florets in a 4 to 6-quart slow cooker.

2. Melt the margarine in a saucepan and add the flour to make a roux.

3. Gradually whisk in the milk, then add the garlic, onion, and cheese.

4. Pour the sauce over potatoes and cover.

5. Cover and cook on HIGH for 3 to 4 hours.

Nutrition Facts Per Serving:

Calories 444, Fat 21g, Carbs 49g, Protein 2g, Fiber 7g, Potassium 1106mg, Sodium 378mg

Prep time: 15 minutes, cook time: 6-7 hours; Serves 6

Ingredients:

- 1lb summer squash, peeled and cubed
- 1lb zucchini squash, peeled and cubed
- ½ cup green bell pepper, chopped
- 1 8oz can unsweetened crushed pineapple
- 1 tsp ground cinnamon
- 1/3 cup brown sugar
- 1 tbsp butter, cut into small pieces

Instructions:

1. Mix all ingredients together and place in a 4 to 6-quart slow cooker.

2. Cover and cook on LOW for 6-7 hours or until squash is tender.

3. Serve immediately.

Nutrition Facts Per Serving:

Calories 113, Fat 2g, Carbs 24g, Protein 2g, Fiber 2g, Potassium 381mg, Sodium 7mg

Slow Cooker Eggplant Lasagna

Prep time: 20 minutes, cook time: 2-3 hours; Serves 8

Ingredients:

- 2 eggplants, peeled and sliced thin to resemble lasagna noodles
- 1 cup low-fat cottage cheese
- 1 ½ cup low-fat mozzarella cheese
- 1 egg
- 1 24oz jar sodium-free spaghetti sauce
- 1 tsp low-sodium salt
- 1 bell pepper, diced
- 1 onion, diced

Instructions:

1. Season the eggplants with salt and pepper, arrange on paper towels and allow excess moisture to drain away.

2. Mix the cottage cheese, mozzarella cheese, and egg in a bowl.

3. Pour ¼ of the tomato sauce in a 4 to 6-quart slow cooker.

4. Layer like lasagna with vegetables, cheese mix, and tomato sauce.

5. Cover and cook on LOW for 2 to 3 hours.

Nutrition Facts Per Serving:

Calories 221, Fat 10g, Carbs 19g, Protein 14g, Fiber 3g, Potassium 349mg, Sodium 802mg